Unseal Your Greatness

NEW YEAR'S RESOLUTIONS THAT
WILL INSPIRE YOU TO LIVE AN
EXTRAORDINARY LIFE

Compiled by **Lauren Brill**
Contributing Writers:

Alacia Thomas, Alexis McWhorter, Angel Woodard, Ashleigh
Ogg, Ashley Kay, Brandi Gomez, Braya Weaks, Briana
Chang, Charmaine Freeman, Danni Hill, Doofanter Iortyer,
Emily Miller, Falencia Buot, Gerald Washington, Gie Santana,
Hamsa, Heather Barnett, Heidi Helena Dunshea, Jejune Ebbs,
Jena Boyer, Jessica Oliver, Joshua Haynes, Josie Pruitt, Lachai
Allen, Magnolia Jojo, Mahogany Roberts, Malak, Mary Jones,
Melanie Tascione, Michael Giles, Mikhala Beckwith, Myjah
Guy, Nicole Gray, Nicole Kisslinger, Ray Whitaker, Reyna
Vasquez, Saba Jobah, Saga Foss, Sarah Perez, Shiana Larocca,
Sonora Cari, Spike Dickerson, Srishti Mishra, Taylor Healy,
Tracy Barnes, Victoria Davidson, Victoria Wynn.

Book Cover by Marija Džafo

Layout Design by Larissa Fleury

2023

ISBN Paperback: 979-8-9888582-0-1
ISBN Ebook: 979-8-9888582-1-8

Index

Introduction

Dear Readers,

Back in 1999, I was just a kid, but I vividly remember all the chatter surrounding the turn of a new century. Some people were planning epic parties, while others hypothesized the end of humanity. Will Smith rapped about the upcoming New Year's celebration, and news stations reflected on history. New centuries, new decades, and even new years are a big deal for many people because they designate a specific time for you to evaluate your life and create a plan for a fresh start. While the truth of the matter is, every day, every moment, you have the opportunity to change your life.

However, since the new year is when most of us reflect, members of The Unsealed community shared poems at the start of 2023 about their goals for the new year. Some are about specific achievements, while others are about a change in mindset. Each one has a thoughtful message and a desire for growth. I hope by reading their work, you are motivated to think about how you can and will progress as your life moves forward.

With love, hope, and faith,

Lauren Brill (The Founder of The Unsealed)

What is The Unsealed?

The Unsealed (**theunsealed.com**) is a writing community where people write, share, and respond to personal and inspirational open letters. We hold weekly writing workshops and conversations, inviting interesting guests to talk to our community about their stories. Our platform aims to heal, empower, connect, encourage, and inspire people to persevere through their problems.

If you would like to see more from any of our authors, you can check out their page by placing their username in this link. "https://theunsealed.com/members/ **username**/"

11

Dedication

13

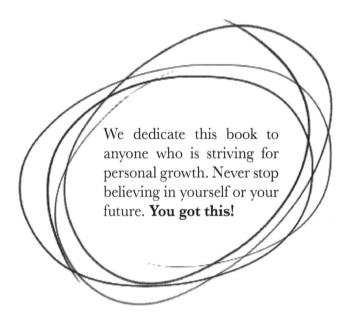

We dedicate this book to anyone who is striving for personal growth. Never stop believing in yourself or your future. **You got this!**

Unseal Your Greatness

NEW YEAR'S RESOLUTIONS THAT WILL INSPIRE YOU TO LIVE AN EXTRAORDINARY LIFE

By Saga Foss
Username: saginthesun

———————

Life Is Lived Better with No Plans to Come

They define a goal as a desired result
A place you could be but you've never felt
A goal is a destination at the end of a journey
The drive that demands and begs you to hurry
So when asked what my goals are my answer is none
Because goal over journey is simply no fun

We scale mountains of wants just to fall down so deep
Not aware that the journey is the thrill that we seek
Eyes blinded by goals and cyclical lists
Ambitions that sink into vicious abyss

We strive so vehemently to reach our goal
Yet it only corrodes a much bigger hole

One so rapacious it can never be filled
A thirst so dehydrating it won't ever be killed
So when asked what my goals are my answer is none
Because what good is a dream if it ever is done?

Why live a life that your past version wrote?
When a life in the present is a life filled with hope
And I prefer not be bound by the constructs of time
Because the longer the journey the finer the wine
So when asked what my goals are my answer is none
Because life is the prize and you only get one

17

We're taught to set goals and strive hard for peace
But goals are a monster that never know sleep
We're taught that success will make us content
Convinced that our failure is a pain we lament
But desire and pleasure are not truly friends
Letting go of desire is when suffering ends

So when asked what my goals are my answer is none
Because life is lived better with no plans to come

Saga

By Ashleigh Ogg
Username: ashes478

———————

18 Love Letter to the Moon

At the darkest of hours, in the deepest of nights
I turn my head upwards, straining to catch sight
Of the brilliant woman who brims with soft light
Overflowing her cup, spilling into the sky

This woman is me, if only I
Had once been strung up as a certain type of Christ
Left there long ago, at the beginnings of time
To serve as a symbol, to serve as a guide

But I am not old, and I am certainly alive
Yet that radiant woman resides in my mind
I aspire to be her, minus the Christ
Without that part I think I'll be fine

She serves as a symbol, deep in my eyes
Her visage engrained until the end of my time
I want to be her, there is no lie behind
The way that I hope to emulate her light

I hope to radiate, on my friends I'll shine
To clear the darkness inside of their minds
I'll take notes from my lover, who turns me blind
To all that which does not deserve my time

I hope to inspire, have people get behind
The visions I have for your world and mine
Together we stand, our hands will unite
With those who choose to stand up and fight

I hope to exist, in between those lines
Before stanza six, but after stanza five
I hope to do everything and nothing in my time
I hope to have everything, to give what is mine

But I cannot do these things if I do not provide
Myself with the love of a lady most kind
If I am to give, I must also resign
To being the first one I choose to admire

Ashleigh

19

By Angel Woodard
Username: thagreatascend

Resolutions in Reflections

I looked at myself in the mirror then heard self say hey
check this out You're 24 now and it's about time you sprout
I see a better future in your fortune
2023 is when you come alive
Sleep visions beyond the tunnel
Time is always on your side
Take those steps confidently in the direction of dreams
The passion behind your purpose
Can you not manifest what you've already seen
No more procrastination we're making it do what it do
Self discipline before self destruct
Through self always stay true
You are what dreams are made of
All goals are nothing but ignited balls of desire

To the greatest from the greatest **spoken** out of honest love
It's already written now time for **all wi**shes to transpire

Angel

21

By Ashley Kay
Username: akay88

_____

22 # Magic Girl

You've got the magic girl
to attract your greatest desires.
Time to let fear go
and allow passion to take you higher.

Follow the affirmations you speak
and watch a love story bloom.
That moment will lead you
to becoming the bride that has finally met her groom.
No longer will you have to wonder
if fairy tales do come true.
Because after you say hello to Prince Charming,
you won't have to guess or try to figure out clues.

Wondering if you are good enough
or worthy of the crown.
The Magic's already inside of you
eyes up, don't look down.

Take a deep breath and exhale
he's waiting for your arrival.
You've already got the magic girl,
And that's final.

Ashley Kay

23

By Brandi Gomez
Username: bgomez

———————

Out of the Water

Dear Self,
I know your happiness comes from creativity.
Your inspiration from the love, the pain and the stories
around you.

You used to have a rhythmic flow that produced often.
That opened eyes to truths and smiles to joy.
That formed tears through idle moments,
and embraced newly introductions.
You used to hold your head high in confidence.
Now your leaving the new year holding it above sea level,
A mark that told me you weren't drowning just yet.
Everything seemed to build up within you,

like you were ingesting the ocean into your lungs.
And without creativity,
your brain was on life support with no activity.

You didn't feel like you were living, just existing.
A floating head in the ocean, just hoping for something.

25

But then a sparkler lit a flame in you
You thought had been lost.
An unconditional promise
you've been praying for
since abandonment at your own cost.

It whispered resolutions that spoke foreign.
That spoke of digging only to fold inside out,
to discover a you that never found an ending.
Just consistent creations in everything that you do.
This is the new chapter I want for you;
To find love and pain inside you instead of around.
To face the beautiful brokenness you always kept hidden.

Dear self, it's time for new inspiration.
Out of the water, the ocean, and into yourself.
Into a new year of rhythmic humility.

Brandi

By Braya Weaks
Username: brayaweaks

———————

New

the two holes in my face
where my eyes used to be
have begun to spread —
my remaining soul begins to leak
and I start to smell the reek.

what reeks I cannot have;
what feels I do not own;
what sings I cannot reach;
i am not my own.
it smells of burnt lust and old fuzz
i start to cough but nothing evades
there's nothing left of me to free
there's nothing left of me that's me.

//

the clock turns twelve
i have my eye drops that I no longer need;
so the eye drops, they seem to fall asleep
the mirror reflects no light; no life
the shower shivers; it hates itself
the tv flickers; a bright baby blue
(or maybe crimson red)

i see the Sea in the hue
or do I see my eyes?
(they used to be bright baby blue too)

//

this dessert you feed me
oh how it eats me;
not I, that eats it
— oh no, not I —
— oh no, I wouldn't dare—
it steals the nourishment I have
it takes
and takes and takes and takes
(this Desert is trapping)
there is wind in my soul
and this fine slender sand makes me cough;

but still, I try to eat it.
it's the only thing I have.
(this Desert is trapping)
you hold my life as an hourglass with slender sand.
your white knuckles withered, strangling my glass
(trapping my Desert)
so

there is no me;
there is no time that is mine
(time isn't yours, but you hold it still)
(sight isn't either, but you carry mine still).

//

Oh look!
The Sea sees me; and I see it too
The lighthouse blinds me; I fall.
The esoteric night sky that they call the Sea
Oh how it eats me!
It's royal blue encases all my crevasses

While the whales feed me to the plankton
I am not what is not me;
But I am just as much food, as food is me.

Oh, but no!
I have been eaten, but have given nothing;
My life as a sacrifice
Is like a lamb without meat;

My bones are brittle,
My heartbeat weak,
But my diaphragm that's ripped out,
It is still singing!

Oh, It starts raining!
What a wonderful sight to see
The rain joins the water; so the rain joins me
Oh new life!
Oh how bright!

The rain seeps through, I am renewed!
The two holes in my face have been filled by the
Sand of the Sea
tears of God
And the resilience of
Me.

//

I didn't find my eyes;
The Earth made another pair for me.
I didn't get my time;
I made time get me.

I didn't reject the food, but ate it;
As food will no longer eat me.

//

my bones form together;
My flesh is flesh no more;
my skin finally breathes;
My brain is back in place;
my back is back up right;

30

Oh what a wonderful day;
oh what a wonderful night!

oh how the clouds blessed me

this new year.

Braya

By Briana Chang
Username: cheechedb

The Goal of a Human Stuck in the Middle Way

You must pick a path today,
So real goals can be made.
It cannot be the Middle Way.

Your enlightenment is not underway.
C'est la vie, I am afraid.
You must pick a path today.

A doctor for my parents to display?
But what if I just want to design bouquets?
It cannot be the Middle Way.
This feels like a human cliche.
Why cannot all desires be attained?
You must pick a path today.

I want to get the earth out of disarray.
But which way? There are many that are paved.
It cannot be the Middle Way.
As I sit by the ocean in Marseilles,
All I want is to lay in the sun and evade.
You must pick a path today.
It cannot be the Middle Way

33

Briana

By Charmaine Freeman
Username: charthepoet

2023

Someone asked me about my goals for 2023.
It's an easy answer, I just want to be a better me.
Continue improving me.

Master the art of self-love, as I cut away the baggage that's
been holding me down. In 2023, I want to forgive myself.
Now is not the time to focus on nonsense or on things that
cause regrets.
Yes, some decisions were for the worst. My own actions
made me hurt. I accept that those decisions had to be made
for things to turn out this way, and that's okay. Because
2022 left no stones unturned. I truly learned. And I'm
ready for what's next. In 2023, I'm stepping into my best.
In 2023, the plan is to live positively.

Provide an environment that is healthy, physically, and emotionally.
For not just me but also for my seed.

2023 is about my daughter. Developing that bond that can be broken by none. She needs to know that she is the one my world revolves around. Surrounding her with love only a mother can provide.
2023 is to make her thrive.

Last but not least, my goal for 2023 is to not let anyone walk all over me.
Self-betrayal is no longer an option. So, a word of caution…negativity will not be tolerated in 2023 or any year thereafter, so don't bring it to me.

2023 is not just for me its for all of us,
To make it better than it was.

My goal for 2023 is for us to spread love rampantly.

Charmaine

By Doofanter iortyer
Username: dauphine

Goals of a Lover

At times I am at a loss for words because
I have this heart that loves so deeply,
A soul that soars and gives so freely,
A spirit that weeps yet knows no bounds,
A journey that tells stories of creation profound.

In this new season all I wish
Is to love abundantly and never cease to relish,
Relish in all my heart knows, to be filled with peace wher-
ever I go.

My journey will bring me so much delight,
As I choose to share my love with all in sight.
I will love this world with my heart and soul,
And bask in the joy in which it unfolds.

Doofanter Iortyer
Dauphine

37

By Emily Miller
Username: wishfulwriter75

Goals for 2023

As I look ahead to 2023,
I think about the person I will be.
Although I am already a wife, a sister, and a daughter,
I want to make life a little rawer.
It often seems I am living for myself,
But I want to stop and ask; what about everyone else?
In a world that's filled with sicknesses and with crime,
I fully aim to be the light!
I want to be the person that people look up to,
Rather than being someone who follows what others do.
As I am given one life altogether,
I aim to be thankful through whatever.

My goal in 2023,
Is to become the best person I can be.
Although I will face challenges along the way,
I want to make an impact that will stay.

Emily Miller

39

By Gerald Washington
Username: lostone89

———————

2023 Is Around the Corner

2023
You stuck up on us
Like deer in the night
I had heard of your coming
But still wasn't prepared for your arrival
At the same time,
I'm excited you'll be at my door soon
There's so much I want to tell you
Hopefully, you won't be overwhelmed
by my words
I want to tell you
That I want to finish my book
Travel to other places
Continue to work on being a better writer

And to pursue it as a career
I also want to strengthen my relationships
and make new ones
2022 went by so quickly
I'm hoping you'll go slowly
As long as your year is a good one
For every human being
and creature on earth

41

Gerald

By Gie Santana
Username: giesantana

---

42   # 2023 and G.I.E.

Hello there sweetheart.
This year, in a nutshell you will simply smile more.
I know last year was quite the doozy and it took a lot of
your essence away, your tenacity and a bit of your umph
away as well. But you pushed through now look at you!
2023! A year you couldn't quite vison a bit ago. But none-
theless a beautiful attest in being champion of your life.
I sincerely want you to smile, unapologetically and loudly.
This year when someone asks, "Are you doing okay?"
You will confidently and accurately say "Yes".
You will beam with joy because this year, in 2023, you
WILL be happy.
How will you do that?
My darling, read on.

Those projects you are working so hard on will flourish and
make room for you in places you have yet to dream of.
You will continue healing, practicing healthy, happy, and
wholesome vibes that ooze out into the world and make you
feel super cozy on the inside.
Inside.
No more major self-isolation. Allow yourself to feel exactly
what you are feeling and embrace it wholly.
You will no longer try on self-scrutiny at clothing stores.
You will instead stunningly step into the best fitting pair of
confidence and acceleration for life there is.
Gie Gie, its 2023!
Your health scares, and constant worries WILL be replaced
with consistent improvements, miraculous mentions, and a
lot of high fives!
You will speak up. Your voice is beautiful, and it shall not
be only made to whimper in this grand life.
It's also made to belly laugh so full you dribble food out in
pure excitement!
So far, you've wrote down 175 goals to accomplish just this
year, big or small and guess what lucky duck? You will get a
Guitar and learn how to strum sweet cords.
I know you've always wanted a guitar. You have been in
constant awe of anyone who knows how to play, plus 2-time
Guitar Hero champion right here, your ready for sure.

You love a fierce cat eye, often hid by your glasses but
learning how to apply basic makeup is a razzle dazzle goal,

43

you plan to trial and error it until your face either screams circus or success.

Depending on the day it could scream both.

You will take more time for self, more time to evolve, nurture the interworking's of self and investing in self.

You will produce zero guilt for taking a day off.

Even if the day off is to lounge and binge watch your favorite cooking show for the hundredth time.

It is allowed.

Gie, you have faced many obstacles. Ones where you were certain you could not move on from.

Each day as the goal list grows bigger, brighter, and even a bit scarier you WILL embrace it and simply do it all with a smile. A smile that is not forced, preempted, or leaves you wondering why.

This year in 2023 Gie you will smile.

And skydive.

Goal 176.

Gie

By Heather Barnett
Username: lavendertulip

For My 2023 Self

Dear 2023 me,

I have some goals I've been wanting to accomplish for the last few years now. Yet I've either haven't had the time or energy to do so. Now I'm leaving them up to my 2023 self to do. I hope they'll get accomplished and fulfilled to my most true self.

To start off with, I loved running in my school years and I could use the exercise. I used to do soccer, track, then swim and dive, but I always had my obstacles I faced and passed, especially during the 300 hurdles in track. I used to feel so carefree and powerful during it. Plus, running was always my favorite thing because it helped me blow off steam from school.

Next, I want to go to college now. I took that needed gap year for a break from the expectations and school burnouts.

I have loved art all my life, so that's what I want to go for and minor in creative writing. That is a little newer interest, but I love doing it. I've never been excited for school, but now I know I'm ready and know what I want to do. I used to not know what I wanted to do in life, and I'm still not fully sure, but I know what I'm good at.

47

Finally, I want to get back into reading again. I always found peace in reading. It was like traveling into the book, seeing, feeling, and hearing what the character was. Reading can help people in more ways than you'd think. It helps teach empathy, improves sleep, reduces stress, increases general knowledge, and improves the ability to focus and concentrate on things. It's also helped me with all these things, so I enjoy reading more now because of it.

Also, 2022 me, thank you. You got me out of some scary places we fell into the last couple of years from everything going on, but my friends, partner, and sisters have helped me a lot too. Just keep going, and let's get mentally better together. I can't wait to see what you accomplish for us in 2023.

– Sincerely,

the past you

Heather Barnett

By Heidi Helena Dunshea
Username: heidihelenadunshea

───────────

The Peace in Your Sky

Dearest,
Last year I clutched close to every piece of home,
Sorting through the numbness with trembling hands.
But the new year's morning is bathed in apricity.
Aliferous and untainted.
So I let myself slip under the bright simple day.
The tempting beauty of just being.
Thoughtful footsteps on holy ground:
A tradition long overdue.
The frankness ruined the folklore;
The nightmare interrupted the epiphany;
Life left the color vulnerable.
It won't always;
I promise.

This callow year has been blessed by your touch.
All I need is to continue quietly,
Under these wandering trees their boughs bent in relief,
Without fear of what has been left behind.
It will come again.
We are forever beginning again.
I'll always be clutching pearls on a string,
But I know who is in control.
I see dewy strands of musical light weaving peace in your
sky.

Heidi Helena Dunshea

49

By Jejune Ebbs
Username: jejune06

_____

New Year's Sun

The snow may come soon
and conceal all that it touches
but like the flowers
that lay buried beneath
I want to be seen

I've moved here from a long way
from a place I couldn't call home
I was not seen there or heard from
I was truly alone
But with snow comes spring
and a horizon of blooming
moments and chance
It's there I will rise out
of the heavy snow and

set forth toward the sun
Through open hands,
I will reach for it and
ask it to shine on my work
and burn it's pages into every
soul who dare stare into
the sun's illuminating flames
I want to be seen
I want the life
I've always dreamed of

Make all the hard and bitter times
worth it until the person I once
was is finally redeemed – done
I write for one purpose and
am desperate to tell a story
So, that in time, I will find
companions of equal standing
and bleeding hearts
to bask in the glory

I wish the new year to bless
me with these things
In return, I give all that I am
My love, I hope by then
you'll still be with me to dance

Jejune Ebbs

By Joshua Haynes
Username: sage-jawsh

The Sagey-Verse

Dear, Sage.

Last year you learned that many fear Sage. Just like many fear age. That this life is like a clear page. That in order for your story to assure glory, one must have a clear stage. And that I'm the twentieth first century there takes many mental trees. Branches that enhance us. That even when the wind leaves. We can breathe. This year is about your triumph. Facing what scare you most, with no need to buy guns. That your intelligence has more relevance than a bill of a duck to the pelican. That your movement has to be more consistent than a peloton especially when you're born with an excess of melanin. Especially when the affliction is as good as your diction. That talk is cheaper than if you were selling tongues. Especially hailing from where the felons are

young. Where the mothers have been accosted by hard-
ships. That inside your heart is where God lives regardless.
You were born to be the spark in the darkness. That your
only real intent is vigilance. That your mind can unlock
the most distilling mixture. That life is what we paint it. A
feeling a picture. That memories are the brail that let's the
read the love that can often blind us. That creation is proof
of what time does until our times up. And you, Sage are a
living story always embarking upon a new page. Looking
for more of yourself like a CLUE game. To be all that you
can be is your true aim. Even despite the fact that behind
your smile that's worth a while. Is an aisle that new pain.
But the same hurt is pivotal in ascertaining the gaining of
true style. This year you use trials and new routes to do you.
That your mission is not to score the goals of other souls but
for your mold to presume glue. The togetherness meant for
you to weather the storms and obstacles that have just go
to go. That you must be like shaolin's profoundness. And
flow. On the road to nirvana, you must earn armor. Not
for battle young warrior but to assure you're tough. That
in this poker game called life. You play your cards right.
And procure bluffs. Not the ones of fallacy but the arboreal
entities that have known to bring winter's scenes. This year
is about adventure and sinking your teeth into things so
deep you wished you had dentures. Through caution to the
wind and your credentials. The conquest for the complex is
quite simple. We all have had locks on our pads and paths.
But to truly succeed in writing your wrongs. All it ever used

53

to take. Was one pencil. You're a child of God at odds with so many who are afraid of the dark. No matter what boat you're in, brother. Never be afraid of your heart. It keeps you with you. So it's safe to say that each day it's meant to may a way for your ark.

Sage

By Magnolia Jojo
Username: magnoliajojo

———————————

Weeping May Stay the Night, But Joy Comes in the Morning

Dear Jasmine,
You have been through so much in your young life. But you've also learned that when life gets you down, you get right back up and you keep fighting the good fight!
It's not easy out here. It doesn't matter if you're rich, poor, black, white, green, or blue; everyone goes through some kind of hardship in their life.
But for you Jazz, the year 2022 has taught you that it is okay to stand up for yourself and it is okay to let go of people you love dearly when you see they are holding you back from what you are supposed to do in life.
For the year 2023, this is about YOU taking back COMPLETE CONTROL of your life, Jasmine! Demanding the respect you deserve and healing your mind, body, and soul!

This will be a long journey but sooo worth it! Pay attention to your body and thoughts and **REJUVENATE!** Cheers to peace, love, and new found happiness in 2023!

Magnolia Jojo

57

By Mahogany Roberts
Username: mahoganyglaze

2023 & Me

2023 what you got for me?
I know this sounds so basic
for me , I just wanna peek,
Inside in my wits, bursting evolution leaks

Exploration of further knowing of my becoming
Awaits me on a cold blizzardy day,
So often do we say " My new year resolution,"
I scream, I CLAIM my REVOLUTION!
How? I want to know now how I will be consistent
With me and not get buried under the cold and
Wintry.
When will I actually begin?
Who Is Invited to this Voyage ?

What does it feel like to live in true love, rest and contentment ?

Okay, Im overwhelming me, *inhales..exhales*

Hey Beautiful, firstly, it did not take me being in a situation-
ship
With that fine brotha to know that I are,
Taking that with Me high and far.
Setting my standards and not lowering the bar,
Open myself up to deeper healing, cause everyone has scars
The How, it's all about my consistency,
I will remember I am becoming even more free!
All throughout my anatomy.
The desire to succeed is burning brighter
than the fire of heartache of past mistakes

Gonna Breathe and reflect on love every chance I get
Grateful for what I have overcome. I may experience more
cold days
On the flip, I am more prepared to bundle and nurture
wearing the boots of peace to not slip.

Climbing inclines, strengthening muscles, cutting extra
weight and
Most of all, treating my body like a sacred temple, replen-
ishing with
Water, fruit all in moderation.

I Want to try new things, like kayak in the spring,
Horseback ride on a beach , See my children continue
smiling
Increase my knowledge in my profession, Dial 988 for suicide prevention
learn that more of this parenting
Is a blessing.

Save that income, buy that tiny home, Frugal yet classy,
minimal yet met necessities
One day at a time, Trusting the Divine. Its gonna be a good
year.

Mahogany

By Malak
Username: malakkc

Intentions

Upon reflection on a year gone by,
I notice that life is short and needs to fly.

As time dissipates in the fog of winter
Storms that flog your optimism into a pauper,

I lie back and wonder …
How do I make the following year better?

My goals are set for my self-improvement,
Where I wish to feel no bereavement.
Goals are so arbitrary, that, at times

They pull you down into hades.

As I set my goals: reducing my intrusive
Conversation and being more conservative

In my opinions, but only with certain
Peoples, who lack perception.

Another goal is too write more,
Submit more, and succeed more.

I believe the latter more feasible,
As the first requires me to be more biddable
I hope to achieve a certain censorship
As not to reach hardship.

Malak

By Mary Jones
Username: maryjones18

The Girl I Wish to Be

Her days start with prayer.
Gratitude drips from her lips.
Her temple is mentally and physically undefiled.
Her most important relationships are well watered and
flourishes even in tribulation.
She's partnered with grace.
She's partnered with purpose. Even the breaths she takes
are
taken with intention.
She's constantly gaining knowledge and peace as she re-
stores the world.
Selfish and selfless.
She's mastered the balance. She caterers to love so when
the time comes for reaping,

they won't forget what she sowed.
She takes her rest seriously.
Making sure to recharge and be the light she was created to
be.

- The Girl I Wish To Be

By Melanie Tascione
Username: karmasdreaming

Holy Grail of 2023

2023 , please be good to me
For all the years add up to thee

May I gain more wisdom to pass around
After all, through actions we're bound

2023, my goals come easy
More peace within my head
No more friends who wish negativity
For a gentle soul better leads unfret

Distinguished at heart I plan to explore me
Dive deep within, 2023

These goals seem witless to some, but to others a dream
After all, loving souls haven't come easy to me

Always growing my proclivity in hopes it can start a domi-
no affect

2023, open up my opportunities without fear of failure
Bring "genuinity" together with adventure

Improving skills embedded deep within me
Open them up and set the belle free
Creating a movement of kindness from one country to me

All this starting with an unadorned act placed unto she
As she Witnessed too much hate at such a young age

May these goals present success, family growth, new dy-
namics along with change
For which we all deserve to a conditional extent

2023, my growth is placed on a pedestal so high
So I ask for the strength to carry them forward
Surrounding myself with those who yearn to eclipse them-
selves
So that the ones I love dearly equally excel
The new companions we meet can all tag along
For this new found growth must be passed on

2023, above all I seek the connection to nature so pure and
so deep
For anyone questioning me is eager to seek
The answer to this world we created
All this and more from a number so highly elated
As a beginning of your own efforts not being demented
Manifestation heeds peace, would you not say?

I beg you, 2023, don't keep these things at bay

2023, please be good to me
For all the years add up to thee

Karma

By Mikhala Beckwith
Username: mikhala

From Visions to Memories!

Dear Mikhala,

This year, you stop getting snubbed. There were too many moments where you stood back, gave your self-expression up for the sake of community, and said "in due time"… well it is due time. When you wake up, you will be in the front of life. No more being hidden in plain sight. Let everybody go blind if it means you keep shining. You see your path, and walk it. You know what to do with your life, and you do all of it. Success comes easily to you, because you make hard work seem easy. You get in that car that you earned, all on your own, drive it to your apartment where you find peace and quiet, and it is just you and your cat Sebastian. Bali, Italy, New York… they will be so happy to see you show up this year. This year, vacation is your friend. You have a great job with great pay, and you don't have to give up your mental health to have it. This is the year that your friends stop by with snacks and wine so good, the re-runs on TV seem extra hilarious! And maybe you will or won't find love this time, but when you ask yourself "will I find love?" the answer won't hurt or make you nervous anymore. It won't hurt to even wonder if you will. You know how to take it one day at a time this year. This year, your vision board becomes a memory board.

I love you, I will never play around when it comes to you,

Mikhala

71

By Myjah Guy
Username: msoul18

_____

Little Letters to Soul

Soul,

I have always found solace in writing to you. I remember I
want, I can, I will. Our lives are more intertwined than I've
previously believed them to be. I have seen your visions and
know they are promises to me. There is so much depth for
me, isn't there? Because I can only feel the vastness of the
universe, not see it. You can see what I can only feel. You
can see my possibilities as a woman, whereas I can only
feel them. A home to care for, pages to build a world, and
to hear my child take her first breath. It is all I could ever
want, know I can have, and will it to be true. By closing
my eyes, my darkness illuminates possibilities. But what are
these realities if not you? Therefore, wouldn't my dream
for the year be to become bonded to you peacefully and

eternally? To caress my mind and become submissive to all of you? I wish to be vulnerable so your words can heal and create. By becoming you it would mean I lack nothing in every moment. To know my dreams are never apart from me but a breath away from my infinite darkness.

Myjah

P.S. My heart no longer wishes to clench itself in order to survive, it hopes to live.

By Nicole Gray
Username: ngray00

From Dreams to Reality

"MASH",
A game I played when I was an adolescent.
A game full of lies but made from dreams.
Funny,
I find myself at that same point in life.
'Wanting so many things but not sure if I will get them.
My dreams,
Keeping a home my parents didn't put in a will but worth saving.
I long to have a family to pass it down to.
Raising them to do the things I've never had the opportunity to.
Like pedaling on four wheels, floating on a body of water or twirling in a pink skirt and flat shoes.

They'll know The Big Apple I grew up in but will love the
city that made my dreams come true. Writing,
A passion I inherited from my mother,
A hobby that will soon be my career.
Being a loner as a child made me create my own verbal
fairytales.
Those fairytales turned into words on a page,
And now those words will be pictured on a big screen.
My healthy family will be there to witness pure
determination.
All of the failures they encouraged me through will lead me
to success.
Twenty Twenty-Three,
Will be the year I conquer the world.

Nicole Gray

By Nicole Kisslinger
Username: nicoleskisslinger

———————

I Will Be Free Soon

Dear Chaos,

I am no longer an anxious, cooped-up vessel,
Trapped inside the mind of my own —
Rather inside the mind of what resembles a stranger's.

Heal, don't hustle.
Flow, don't force.
Ground, don't grind.

Seasons have passed;
My body is safe now.
Breaking free of my once worst thoughts,
Setting me loose to feel and not fight.

I am receiving all of what makes me, me.

I am no longer doing, I am being.
I am no longer chasing, I am attracting.
I am no longer anxious, I am secure.

I am safe in this body and in this brain.

77

From,

Calm

By Ray Whitaker
Username: whitjr

———————

Dialogue with Myself Towards 2023...

There is time you spent looking
somewhere in the course of the day
or days
or weeks and months
maybe even years
for that certainty of presence.
This is where you are no longer any sort
of impostor
of fearful
of lacking
of emotional
or dramatic
when the only thing there is, is that you, yourself, are.
those noises in your head are you

however not you
the illumination from introspection is many thousands of
years old
from the masters it is possiblc to experience
the presence of who you are being
there is a grayness before the shining bright white
the smell of this work is the odor of freshly cut grass
and the sense of it, is that what you are looking for, is no
longer missing.
That what was missing was always there, even so.

Ray Whitaker

By Sarah Perez
Username: sarita

2023 and Me

I want you to breathe easier
To not critique yourself and art into artistic paralysis
Do not question your Intuition
I will let you make mistakes
Only if you can learn from them
I will not beat you up for being human

I will give you the grace I allow others
I am now able to love you as you need to be loved.
And that love will grow with each passing day

I believe that you are worth the struggle.
That love is just as important to receive as give.
You will be the change you want to see in this world.
You will rage against the dying light
And I will love and be proud of you with every moment of
this coming year.

Sarah

By Shiana Larocca
Username: shianajasmine

———————

You Are Beautiful

Life is a beautiful lie,
Your told not to cry,
To move on and wipe your eyes.

A butterfly becomes a butterfly by its wings,
The same goes for any seed that plants a tree.

A drop of rain that turns into a river,
A smile that turns into a laugh.

Leaves fall just like I fall for you.

Beauty is in the eyes of the beholder,
Or so I've been told.

Love is as deep as magic in a bottle,
Shedding the old to experience the new.

A life is as simple as a book,
Some pages must be written,
And Some pages must be ripped out.

Don't you see the beauty that lies within you?

The change and growth that emerges out of you,
The light that surrounds you,
The love that's inside of you.

You see two sides to you in the mirror,
Not just the good and the bad,
But the old, and the new.
You see and feel the change all around you.

The world is a dangerous place to love,
but it is also the best place to learn,
to discover who and what we are at the core.

To be in the now with every breathe,
feeling at ease, and at peace.

It's more simple than we all make it out to be.

We are all beautiful creatures,

We just experience the ugly.

You learn,
Memories fade,
just like a leafs in the wind,
Blowing away and never to be seen again.

You learn,
Things aren't always as they seem,
Black and white fading at the seams.

You learn,
Life is about finding yourself,
To learn the truth about who you are,
Within the means.

You learn,
The reality of things have all become a lie,
To ensure people don't wake up,
To the truth of the divine.

Life is a beautiful lie,
But it is also beautiful when you look on the inside.
When you realize things with new eyes.

Beauty comes in many forms,
But true beauty lies within.
It's not just skin deep, it's the norm,

It's the way you treat others,
With kindness and grace.
It's the way you help the world,
And put a smile on their face.

It's the way you face your fears,
To the very end.

It's the way you stand through the storms,
It's the way you dry your tears,
Of those who are feeling worn.

It's the way you speak your truth,
With honesty, and with care.

It's the way you spread your youth,
And show the world you're there.

So don't let the world define you,
What true beauty is,
Remember, you are divine,
And all that you need is to see that
you are beautiful on the inside.

Cheers to a new year,
and a fresh start,
A beginning that brings a happy end.

85

A chance to start over,
to be a better person.

To think more clear minded,
to nourish the mind, and soul.

To move through the body in a new way,
to take all of the past away.

I'll be more alive and happy,
by being my best self, and changing my ways.

I will raise my spirit to the highest of highs,
I'll take it one day at a time,
And make my future truly sublime.

Life is a beautiful lie,
But the true beauty lies inside,
A shining star so bright,
And with that inner beauty as your guide,
You'll be a beacon of light.

Shiana Jasmine

By Sonora Cari
Username: sonora

———————

In the New Year

Right now, there is snow on the ground and children sled
down the big hill in the park,
Shriek out in joyous rapture

From the window:
smells of rosemary, bacon sizzling in the pan, and coffee
burnt but loved by all fathers who share in the exhilaration
of a snowy day

Today is filled with happiness, shared as commonly as the
lone cigarette at a party,
Passed around

Still, and not unlike that cigarette, the day is filled with a
feeling of finality

Heavy as led
When it is over,
When the clock strikes for the last time, feeling more like a
pcriod than a comma
Ball dropping in Times Square like that most final form of
punctuation

That is when I wonder:
What will those children's delighted screams sound like in
the next year to come?

Will the fathers hope for more wind chilled days where
their young cry out to be pulled along in that red toboggan
we all know so well?

Do they wish for their children to call out to them, "please
daddy, please just one more ride!" as they watch their ba-
bies grow?

I may never know what those fathers, those proprietors of
black and bitter folgers, wish for when they hear that vast
and final toll of the clock tonight, marking the end of their
latest sentence

And what of the children?
Whatever they wish must stay unknown to me, their own
desires a mystery for them alone to learn

And when it rings in at midnight, the clock will have already accomplished it's most sacred task of the year, only wishing to do it again and again endlessly

Comma after comma until the night when the ball drops again
Party poppers exploding in primary colored cheer
The clock ringing out,
A period to end the sentence

When the clock tolls
Heavy
Final
period after an endless run-on
I will hope for just one thing

I will close my eyes
And make a wish:

Love without fear is what will ring in my ears like the music all around me

When I feel myself grow angry, stubborn, or closed off
Love without fear is what will bring me back
this year

I can taste that goal like candy hearts, passed out in grade-school Valentines

When I turn on the news to see fires
Or war
Or violence of unspeakable measure
Those horrible unmentionable things that make blood boil

I will still look out my window and see love in all that's
around me

Keep candy hearts under my tongue so even the most bitter
days taste sweet

And I will have love this year

Love for my students
And friends
Love for my own mistakes
Love for forgiveness, and the planet, and the oceans and the
heavens above

Love
For all of it

I will hear that bell ring, twelve booming dings
And I will have only one shining syllable roll around on my
tongue
That word will break free from my mouth in a joyous shout

The ecstasy of newness will overtake me then, and I will

begin the hard work of loving myself,
Of loving the things I cannot change

I will do this so that maybe the next time there is snow on
the ground,
And the bacon,
And the sleds

A period ready to be placed neatly at the end of this sen-
tence, and a clock ready to strike
All around will be the taste of love

Then, with candied sweetness on my breath, I will be ready
with a new list of goals to accomplish
Things far more tangible than this one thing I must do
when the ball drops tonight.

Maybe,
I'll finally learn to sew, or paint, or start a garden

I'll tell strangers how beautiful they are, and walk more, or
learn to juggle, or learn to cook

I will bake the perfect soufflé, and learn new songs, and
write the most eloquent poems

Again,
The clock will ding
And the ball will drop

And people will scream out in glorious cries of "I love you!"
to anyone willing to listen

And there will be confetti, and kisses, and rosy cheeks filled
with grapes for good luck, and happiness radiating from
every direction as champagne is poured, and toasts are
made to good health
And I will have beautiful new goals,
Because

after love all else will follow

Sonora

By Srishti Mishra
Username: srishti

A Letter to Myself About the Goals for the New Year

Dear Srishti,

I am welcoming 2023 with a cheerful smile and a lot of fantasies, and I want them to come true this year. My goals are not so big, the first and foremost goal is to take good care of my family and myself so that I can put all my focus on other goals.

I want to satisfy all my desires and would like to explore new places in India and I would love to travel to other countries e. Travelling is the best remedy to relax your mind and to take short breaks from frenzied jobs.

I shall read some good books which will help me to strengthen my writing skills. I want to write a good short story by the end of 2023. I find it so peaceful to put your thoughts on paper - whatever you are feeling inside, this is one of the finest ways to express feelings and emotions. I know that dreams don't come true overnight, and it will take effort. There are many steps you need to take to reach the destination, but I will try to put my efforts in the right place so that I can achieve at least the first step.

Also, I want to promise myself that I won't waste 2023 at all as I am a little idle sometimes and it's difficult for me to get out of my comfort zone. So, I must wake up and push myself as this is also key for me to have a happy and healthy year.
Looking forward for a joyful 2023
Yours,

Srishti

By Victoria Davidson
Username: victoriamd

———————

Everything I'm Scared of Hoping For, but I'm Hoping For Anyway

Dear 2023 Victoria,

Hope is just the other side of fear. I know that's why you hate to do it, and I understand that. But I'm going to do it for you, for the both of us, for just a little bit. For just the few minutes it takes you to read this letter. And then all I want you to do is carry my hope with you. Deal?

I hope this is the year we really start recognizing our strength. I hope this is the year we start recognizing how f****** hard we work and stop beating ourselves up for everything we don't do. I hope this is the year we start beating our body down less and start giving it credit for everything it does for us, even though it's sick and it's tired and it's hard to live in it. I hope this is the year we start seeing through the disability and the dysmorphia to how beautiful we actually are. Because we are.

I hope this is the year we find the energy, focus, and motivation to make ourselves happy. I hope we find some peace. And some excitement, and some drive to do what we actually want to do, and some real, bright f****** happiness.

97

I hope this is the year we stop finding the idea of real happiness exhausting.

And sleep. I hope we get all the f******* sleep this year. I hope this is the year we stop giving the things that keep us awake at night so much power.
I hope this is the year we find a way to make easy, f****** amazing pho at home so we can have it whenever we want. Or that this is the year we win the lottery or bag a sugar daddy so we can have pho whenever we want. Either way, I hope for pho for us this year.
I hope this is the year we start listening to and believing ourselves when we tell ourselves what we want. I hope this is the year we start knowing that there is actually a point to working towards the things we want, and not just the things that will pay our bills.
I hope that this year we're able to cry again. And not just when we hit our breaking point but every time we feel a deep sadness. I hope this is the year we start feeling deep

sadness again instead of numbness. I hope this is the year we start being able to feel all our emotions again, even the ones we only need to feel so that we can get through to the other side of them. Especially those.

I hope this is the year we start being less alone. I hope this is the year we start really letting ourselves get close to people. I hope this is the year we start actually wanting to be less alone.

I hope this is the year we find out why we've convinced ourselves that we really just want to be alone.

I hope this is the year we find something that makes next year a new galaxy we can't wait to explore instead of an endless expanse of space we have to trudge through.

I can't wait to see what that something will be.

I love you.

And I'm proud of us for hoping.
Sincerely,

2022 Victoria

By Hamsa
Username: vvgrey_

Resolutions

Dear Hamsa,

Remember, I want this year to be authentic for you. Keep your vision of not allowing the world to define you, but to define yourself in the world.

Below is a poem you wrote the last time you believed existence was worth something to love again. Allow these words to be an incantation for what you desire this year:

I want life to continue holding me as its last breath,
its body that was birthed from my womb with wings
as I explore the universe in my mind
and how many lives it holds within its eyes,

worshipping love as law,
and its peace – a temple of miracles.

Hamsa

By Jena Boyer
Username: jenawrites

2023: New Year, Confident Me

As I stroll into 2023
I have high hopes and a positive view
I think of that phrase: "New year, new me"
And if I stay focused, that can be true

It's not that I want to change who I am
I am actually starting to love myself
It's that I finally see my potential, and damn...
I deserve a life full of good health and wealth

I get to decide what I consume
Both physically and mentally
And if I eliminate the doom and gloom
The love and light are what I'll see
This year I will put effort into being present

I will practice the art of letting go
This year, there is no room for resentment
I do what pleases me, and I don't feel guilty saying "no"
As the years go on, I always remain grateful
The hard times and life lessons help me grow
As I get older, I become more graceful
I stand in my confidence as I go with the flow

I am happily floating into 2023
I have faith that all is unfolding as it should
This year I deserve to focus on me
And do everything that happy, healthy me would.

Jena

By Jessica Oliver
Username: joliver15

3M's – Millionaire

Mucho gracias.
Muncho dreams.
Magnificent reality.

Nothing comes to a sleeper but a dream.
Hard work beats talent if talent does not want it as bad as me.
All eyes on me.

I have prayed, prepared, then believed in myself.
It is 2023 and I would not want to be any place else.
I came out my shell,
Learned things not for sale,
The best thing in life is to be yourself.
Life may get tough and beat you up.
No matter what, TRUST the process.

Focus on the good, not the bad.
Be grateful for the future, present, and past.

It could always be worst,
Heal from hurt,
Never lose hope.

Always leave room for growth.
Knowledge is power, which requires evolving learning, you know?
It is 2023 I am still the same Old' me.
I aim to be better every day,
Give to others more then I take.
I am happy with the way I live my life, I can say.
I would not want it any other way.

Continue having faith and patiently wait.
Your dreams are about to turn into reality.
Hard work forever pays.
Greatness is your destination. Destiny is your preservation.
The moment that you are waiting for will come to past, watch and see.
When it does, you are going to laugh and say, "It was worth it, at last, I see!"
Millionaire status
I am very thankful.
I have big dreams.
I will live a magnificent reality

Jessica

By Josie Pruitt
Username: josiepruitt7

Try. Grow. Unfreeze.

Dear Josie,

It's finally over, the dreaded year of 2022. Now you live in 2023, and I hope that this time around, It'll be nicer to you. January of 2022 was the last time you were "Normal." It was the last time you had confidence, love in your heart, and energy. I know you weren't expecting to wake up that Wednesday with the most horrible fatigue and balance issues. Or the way your speech slurred and spoke slowly as if your brain was shutting down. I know we were terrified when our nervous system worked incorrectly, our heart began to beat out of control, and the worst, when we had that seizure.

I want us both to acknowledge the fear it gave us. As I write this letter, I have realized I still haven't processed what happened. In January we had no clue what was happening to us and wondered if when we went to sleep if we would wake up again. Doctors did not know what was wrong, and we felt angry in a struggle that seemingly no one understood. It was the most lonely we had ever been. However, we have answers now. We have doctors who believe us. 2023 is another chance to live our life again, it may not be the same as it once was. But it's better than never getting another chance. As we head into 2023, I want you to do three things for me: Try. Grow. Unfreeze.

Throughout your years at college, you often kept to yourself, especially in 2022. You had some friends, but as time went on, you felt like you lost them. You sat alone in the cafeteria, sang "Happy Birthday" to yourself in your dorm room, and worked all on your schoolwork with no social life. You were isolated, not by anybody, but by yourself. You assumed no one would care about you. But Josie, you were wrong. This year, we are going to "Try". You will take that step out of your bubble and truly reconnect with those friendships. You will try your best to make friends again, and understand that they do love you. We may not succeed all the way, and that's okay. Your legs may wobble and your speech may stutter, but it's a step. When that happens, be proud.

As we went through the year of 2022, you had to withdraw from four classes. Two of which, mean that you weren't going to graduate on time. Throughout 2022, you never gave yourself a break. Each moment was just you badgering yourself, wondering if you were overreacting about what your body was going through. I want you to "Grow" in giving yourself grace. I want you to grow in understanding that dropping those four classes was what was best and that all you could do in those moments was survive. Those naps were needed, and those Doctor visits were too. Josie, none of it was your fault. You weren't overreacting. This year, we are going to let ourselves get rest. We are going to realize when it's time to stop studying our Music Theory homework and make time to spend with others. You are going to do all of this, and not feel bad about it. Because we cannot "Grow", without giving ourselves grace in between.

Lastly, I want you to "Unfreeze". I want you to take your heart out of the cooler, and thaw it out with the bright sunshine that comes from the Kentucky sky. I want your heart to not be numb from the traumatic experiences your health caused you. This part will be extremely hard. It will be hard to love living life again. So- I want our Inner Child, Little Josie to step forward. I want you to remember how badly she wanted to study Music in school, and how excited she is to finally be doing it. Or how much she loved stuffed animals and the fact that we still love them today. Think about how much she loved arcades. I want you to remember her because as our heart froze we never let her step forward again. I wonder maybe if we unfreeze how helpful she could actually be. She was young, but she knew a lot for her age. She knew how to live life despite all the scary stuff. I don't know about you, but man, I miss her.

On a computer screen, this may not seem like a lot. Try. Grow. Unfreeze. Three simple words, right? Wrong. These words will tear us down, it will make us fearful. It will make us question things. But the truth is that we have hit rock bottom. We got our friendships taken away because we let our self-esteem control us. We lost our ability to believe in ourselves because of the after-effects of all our health issues. We lost Little Josie because Big Josie didn't have the energy to care anymore. So- all this is to say, fight. Fight with everything you have left in you because you deserve to live life. When you can't stand, crawl. When you can't crawl, pull yourself. When you can't pull yourself, scream. If you need a reminder of why we need to fight, think of Little Josie.

Because she loves you so much and is so utterly proud of you.

-Love you always,

Josie

By Danni Hill
Username: dannicatwhiskers

Dearest Future Self

Dearest Future Self,

We have many things to look forward to for this new year.

First, there are many changes this coming year. I hope you're wearing a gown and a diploma in your hand by the end of the year. I took my time in community college. It wasn't a race on who could finish their major faster, but I hope you will have your Associate Degree in Health Science. Trying to get straight As in those anatomy and physiology classes wasn't easy, so you better frame that diploma when you get it.

Secondly, I hope you get accepted to that university I never thought you would attend in a million years. I thought that university was a pipe dream. Something pretty to gaze at but unattainable to reach with our hands.

I get so giddy watching reruns of Felicity, Gilmore Girls, and Sex Lives of College Girls. I want so badly to live in a dorm, experience the taste of college life, and just enjoy the freedom of only worrying about my own well-being.

Thirdly, as always, money is a big issue. I hope we find a way to pay for tuition and the dorm. More than anything, I want to experience campus life. Hopefully, the school will offer me a scholarship, or financial aid will be kind to us because I'm also excited to decorate the dorm.

Finally, the last goal that I hope we reach for 2023 is not to let the monstrous beast known as anxiety bring you down. Please keep reminding yourself of how much you have accomplished. You're alive and well, and you're living the life how you want to!

Much Love. I am proud of you.
Your wonderful Past-Self

Danni

By Lachai Allen
Username: lachaibrandii

_____

The Change You Wanna See

"New year new me" they say
Hmm? That makes me think what's new?
It's a new year just a new day really
A new me evolves infinitely
I don't need a year or special day of the week
To show the new in me.
See what I learned from last year was that the year doesn't
change me ?
Now, you see it's the power within me;
It's the conscious choice to prevail against the odds even
when you get weak.
See what I learned from last year is you can say "new year
new me" but if you still around the same people doing the
same things there really want be NO new me, just the same

me doing the same things with the same people still chasing
after the same dreams that I cant seem to grasps
But with true CHANGE I learned you will see what truly
lasts
A new me is born into you
And you
And you
Because when I become new we all do
See that's the true power in being YOU!
When you choose to be the same everything remains the
same
When you choose to change everything around you changes
too
So, if you learned any lessons from 2022 it should've been
the change is within YOU .

113

"Let's Change "New Year New Me" into Let's Be The
Change That We Wanna See."

Lachai Brandii

By Michael Giles
Username: michaelrenee11

M.O: My Letter Thanking the Me in 2023

Dear,
My most divine and optimized being I am so grateful for
You
Each and every day
Breaking free from The Chaos The Heart Ache
and
The Social Restraints
Staying true to
Your
Divine ethereal youth
I am so very proud of
You
I am proud of
Your

Bravery
Your
Ability to choose
You
While addressing the trauma
You've
So long been oppressing
For this is the year

You've
Finally released
Released
Every Physical Mental
and
Spiritual Tragedy   '
This is the year I get to thank
Me
For consciously choosing to step into My
Highest being
An Ethereal Goddess
What some may call a
Masterpiece
What I've always been put in this world to be
A starseed committed to evolving
Effortlessly and consciously
For the growth
You've
Showed me
And ease at which

You
Manifest the life
You've
Always dreamed
Is truly inspiring
It is how
I
Know
I am
A powerful and strong starseed
Placed on this earth to do something bigger than Me
My
Mission serves
justice and peace
For this is
My
Divine Calling
2023,
Thank You,
for never straying away from
Me
Rather,
Vowing to finally show up as
My
Truest most Divine being
Brought here to teach
Selflessly
That this world deserves

more
Happiness Love and Genuine Peace
Just like the heart in
Me.

Michael Giles

117

By Falencia Buot
Username: carmelbythesea

2023

Here are my desires
For 2023
I'll say what my goals are
I'll say my hopes and dreams

I hope to be more open
I hope to find friends to meet
Ones who see the true
and genuine side of me

I wish to put myself out there
To start a new journey
To try new things
And show the world my talents

And my love for poetry

Inside my mind
I hope for peace inside
To nurture my mental health
And dance without a care
Even if it's just in my kitchen
Or anywhere

Lastly, I'd like to discover
What lights a fire in my heart
To become more of who I am
I'd love this year to start
Start going after my passions
And smile in the process
Making mistakes and rising above
Living in my ultimate potential
My ultimate best

Falencia

119

By Saba Jobah
Username: saba

_____

My Year

I wake up staring at my ceiling
My depression whispers that it'll be the same
My anxiety squeals that it'll be worse
But neither my woes nor fears are my eyes
I am a passionate woman with vision
A united community gives me a mission

I wake up staring at my ceiling
My depression whispers that it'll be dull
My anxiety squeals that it'll be pitiful
But neither my woes nor fears are my spirit
This year will be my year to be Ibn Battuta
For I strut with the spirit of a fiesta
I wake up staring at my ceiling

My depression whispers that it'll be overbearing
My anxiety squeals that it'll be troubling
But neither my woes nor fears are my pride
I dream of endless possibilities
Because I know of my abilities
This is my year to claim
It doesn't belong to my depression or anxiety to maim
My eyes, spirit, and pride are the way to my aim

121

Saba

By Spike Dickerson
Username: spikeyda

———————————

I Need $15,000 to Get Through 2023

I understand I'll never make it anyway, but I want to try..
I keep seeing myself as an adult, but then there's yet another
setback or jarring noise
to claw me back, to make me cry..
A woman froze to death in her car?..
How am I to survive when even a glimmer of hope is so
far?..
A husk was all that left my second quarantine of the year..
I thought I'd be fine keeping the weeping's material sheer..
The thoughts were best hidden silently tailored into my
schema..
But I still freak out every time I feel the edema..
But the pain leaked through my eyes and it didn't stop..
Not until it drenched my top..

I just need $15,000 to get through 2023.
You think you've seen horror?..
Wait until you see me gush blood just to be the better scorer..
I just need a couple bandz a year to get me through..
I can't work a regular job, this we already knew..
I don't want to work a regular job, my toes tend to turn blue..

123

Why isn't a plan for my life easily spelled out on me, if it's all pre-ordained?..
I've tried tattoos, but between the design and placement: just the deciding got my limbs chained..
Speaking of tries for perfection and all things predestined,.
all I saw of this world were the Simpson's projections..
Even then, what were we supposed to do with the future in front of our eyes?..
When we all just sit around and glare, we get used to the lies..
The "everywhere audience" thinks it's a better spectacle when one of us writhes..
For 2023 I project prosperity..
I need money, so I'll make it..
I want love, so I'll just take it..
Financial prosperity is the lowest I'll go,.
Any less than that and they wouldn't even consider me, a low-born,
a show..
Maybe I'll fly under the radar..

Even though it's hard to shout-out problems with
repercussions..
Maybe I'll do my best to buy a car..
It's harder to say for sure when toting multiple concussions..
My life/rebellion parallels more to a blaming for the one
percents' misdeeds,.
Even they can't stand the shaming.

for a system that bleeds..

Spike Dickerson (they/them)

By Taylor Healy
Username: tealy

———————

New Year, It's Me

2023
it's time to put the pen to paper
ashes to dust
pour your heart out
with a cup, that isn't half full
because you
can change your surroundings
to be full
even when people try to bring you down

you will change your environment
with the energy inside you
and make life full
even when it pokes

at your very existence
to drain you
to deplete you
to hurt you
and it just might
hurt you

but it won't be like the past
because you are different
the world may flip
open signs to closed
when you approach it
or force you to take detours
without doing anything constructive
but you will heal
you will love
and you will make this year
the best one yet

because you have welcomed death
inviting it to your home
invited it in your heart
to stop the pain
and suffering

you thought this
was a free country
that cruel and unusual

punishment would not exist
but i guess you
learn things the hard way

this year you will live
this year you will be free
not because the world

made it easy for you
my dear
but because you deserve it

you will heal your broken heart
you will be free
and feel like yourself
i love you
until death knocks on the door
not to do us part
but to continue being a part of
the universe in a new way
though it has been bittersweet
my dear
and you want more for yourself this year
you are already home.

Taylor

By Alexis McWhorter
Username: Alexisjanine

The Road I Am Walking

This road im on
It's a wild ride
But I'll keep riding until Dawn
Pushing into being an adult
I try to make wise choices so that I see the result
Reminding myself daily it's alright to be full of love
In a sparrow world, I can continue to be a dove
Confusing as it may be;
I still desire consistency
I choose to make myself proud and others as well, my
improvements shall be loud!
You will make it…
I will make it!
Telling yourself in the mirror so to your changes you must
commit.

The goals may change but the outcome shall remain the
same.
To believe in thy self
But remain humble as to not put myself on the top of the
shelf.
Never let emotions lead the way, for going forward on the
path is how it has to stay.

I never fit in with girls my age, always dared to be different,
But I have slowly learned that is actually magnificent.
I was once told by someone looking into my eyes I would
never be enough,
Little did they realize that would allow me to rebuff
To reach my potential and accelerate is what I choose to do,
For my dreams I want to pursue.
Seeing my patients pass away with the summer in their
eyes,
I remember their spirit flies.
For God I shall live,
For myself I have to give.
I will not give up on myself again,
That's why I have this pen.
The words I write,
Pour out from my heart and I want to shine the light.
Not only for myself but for all who choose to listen.
My future I strongly wish to glisten.

Alexis McWhorter

By Alacia Thomas
Username: Ala

Twenty Twenty Me

here's to a year
of feeling lighter
of practicing
& only pursuing the things
that set my soul on fire.

here's to a year of intentionality
of manifesting my truest reality
and not settling for anything in "actuality"
here's to a year of "no"
of no longer feelings afraid of taking my time
and moving slow.
– slow, intentional movements are the only way we can
grow.

but also,
here's to a year of "yes!"
of falling in loving
of trying to not add to my own distress
by avoiding the things that make me feel best.

here's to a year of authenticity
of simplicity
of consistency
and only engaging in actions
that will lead to my prosperity
and ending 27 debt free.

133

here's to no longer denying my humanity.

here's to another year of peace
but in this one,
I will fully trust
and leave
indecisiveness
worry
and inaction
in tomorrow's dust.

Alacia

By Reyna Vasquez
Username: reynanicole131

This Is the Year

This is the year I learn to breathe underwater
When the tides threaten to overrun the shore and drag me
in
When the waves blanket me and try to swallow me whole
Not knowing
This year is the year I grow gills
I grow fins to help me glide through the water
Because the floaties I had last year popped
And I could only hold my breath for so long
But still- I will evolve

This is the year I learn to fly
When the world tries to tie me down
When the wind makes me a kite on a string

I'll cut myself loose
Turn into a paper plane and soar
Pray the rain doesn't try to ground me
But still- I will endure

This is the year I transform
But still- my roots remain
When my mom cries, I will hold her
When my dad despairs, I will bring him laughter
When my brother worries, I will bring him understanding
However, no longer will I play the martyr
Because this is the year I will only give what I can and not
all that I am
But still- I will love

Reyna

By Victoria Wynn
Username: phillipswynne

_____

Some Advice for You

- Let time go by
Be aware that it'll fly
Just promise me
You'll take it all in
And leave some space to see
How happy you are now
-Take a minute to allow
Yourself the win
To begin again
Don't try to dispute
There's no limit
To the route
In which you drive
I just know you'll thrive.

- Don't follow the clock
Like a watched pot
You'll never get what you want
Or keep what you thought
Was meant for you
It's not all talk.
- But most of all
As this last call
Remember me
And all that we used to be

Victoria

By Tracy Barnes
Username: poeticaddiction_365

---

138 # 2023: Me VS. Me

Dear Tracy,

It's a new year and it's time to focus on you
Whether it's saying no
Or taking a mental health day
You know how to please you
This year is all about elevation
Get to focusing on your goals
To be more productive
With your purpose
Didn't you quit your job last year
To free up time?
Keep in mind
Everything will align

As divine as you are
Sharing your words with others
Will prove to be beneficial
As you find joy in the things you love
This year can be so crucial
As you continue to heal
From your past traumas
There is no need to stress
Live each day
As if it's your last
And do your very best
Don't forget to strive for excellence
And continue to make your mom proud
Being yourself
Will make your heart smile
As practicing self care
Is high on your list
The only thing I'm worried about
Is my main priority
For 2023
I'm not shifting my focus
Cause it's me Vs me
No need for no apology!

Tracy Barnes

139

we hope you are inspired by our letters and poems. If you would like to read more, or share a letter or poem of your own, head to >>

TheUnsealed.com

About the Unsealed Founder, Lauren Brill

Lauren Brill is a seven-time Emmy-nominated and AP-award-winning journalist. Throughout her tenure as a television broadcaster, she worked as a sports anchor and reporter for the ABC affiliate in Cleveland, the CBS affiliate in Buffalo and MSG Varsity in the New York metropolitan area. Also, she has written features for several nationally-known outlets, including NBA.com, WNBA.com, NikeWomen.com, ESPN's Girl Mag and womensprosoccer.com.

143

In 2019, she combined her skills as a writer and television journalist to create The Unsealed. She ghostwrites The Unsealed's featured letters, provides commentaries and hosts a weekly interactive show called Unsealed Conversations. People Magazine, ESPN, ABC, The New York Post and E! Online are among the outlets that have acknowledged The Unsealed's work.

At Columbia University, Lauren majored in sociology, focusing her studies on the impact of sports on society.

Acknowledgments

I want to thank all of our contributing writers. Your truth can and will change the world.